DREAM

NO MORE EXCUSES!

A STEP-BY-STEP GUIDE TO ACHIEVING YOUR GOALS!

An Sean Fields

Dream: A Step-By-Step Guide To Achieving Your Goals!
Copyright © 2018 by An Sean Fields

ISBN 0-9791976-5-1

Printed in USA

DEDICATION

This book is dedicated to my mother, Paulette Y. Fields, AKA "The Cake Lady". It was her dream to own a restaurant but money, fear and the security of her job, kept her bound to cooking and baking out of her outdated kitchen in Jersey City, New Jersey. Even after being featured in the Jersey Journal newspaper for building an entire gingerbread village which included a gingerbread dollhouse with miniature furniture, she still didn't have the courage to pursue the dream. She was truly talented but her gifts were buried with her on April 21, 2006.

It is for that reason, everything I do is in pursuit of my dream. I refuse to let the dream die and allow my family to bury it with me. Instead, I've made up my mind to put away every excuse and focus on my purpose. I've made up my mind when people speak of me, they're going to say, "She died pursuing what she loved!"

I'm also thankful for my daughter, Amani Y. Fields, who is following in my footsteps of letting nothing hold her back from her dream. I pray for every goal and aspiration to manifest in a mighty way. May God bless you and catapult you into a successful career.

To all the dreamers, keep dreaming and don't stop until you've obtained the success you're seeking. There's a light at the end of the tunnel but you won't discover it if you give up. So, hold on!

TABLE OF CONTENTS

INTRODUCTION

One day as I was walking down the street with my daughter and somehow, we got on the conversation of my accomplishments. Them being very few, you would have thought the conversation would've been extremely quick but instead, I began to go on a rant of all the things I want to do, places I want to go and cultures I want to experience. My daughter looked me in the eyes and said, "You're a dreamer!" I took an issue with that statement because she didn't call me a dreamer like it was a good thing but as if I was wasting my time. She said it with such discontent and strong understanding that I wasn't getting any younger and time was quickly ticking away as I stayed stationary in "dream mode."

Dream mode is a state of thinking about what you want to do instead of just doing it. As the conversation began to wind down, I questioned myself. Was the short list of accomplishments not enough to prove that I'm more than a dreamer? Had I given up on reaching for the next level and now stuck in one place? What was it going to take for me to go to the next level? Why did I stop pursuing my dreams in the first place?

> Dream mode is a state of thinking about what you want to do instead of just doing it.

Merriam Webster Dictionary defines a dream as a strongly desired goal or purpose; a vision. For the past few years, the latest trend has been vision boards. Many believe if you can envision it, then you can achieve it. This is partially true. They spend days or weeks, cutting out pictures and words to accompany or represent their dream, and then paste it on a board. This is an attempt to turn the dream or vision into something tangible, something outside of your mind and in front of you that can be touched. Although my accomplishments were achieved without a vision board, I most certainly had a vision. I knew I wanted to turn my daily blog into a book. I didn't have any idea what the cover was going to look like or how long the process was going to take but I knew the only way to turn my vision into reality was by faith.

The bible defines faith as a substance of things hoped for, the evidence of things not seen - Hebrews 11:1 (KVJ). In order to pursue your dreams, you're going to need just a little bit of faith and building enough faith to pursue your dreams require courage. Neither a dream nor faith begin as something tangible, in which you can touch and hold in the palms of your hands but if you believe hard enough and take all the appropriate steps you can see both dream and faith manifest.

A quick way to jump start your faith is to ask yourself, "What do you have to lose?" Seriously, I really want you to look around at your current situation, your bank account, your resume, your current employment status and ask yourself, "What do you have to lose at this point in your life?"

The first business I started with a group of co-workers failed – it didn't work. We had an idea, we came together, rented some space and got busy but it failed because of so many issues, however, we had the courage to at the very least try. We made an attempt to create something out of absolutely nothing. I cherish that experience because it taught me what not to do, to partner with people of like mind and how to move forward in business. One of my former business partners pushed pass that failure and is now a successful entrepreneur working full-time for herself. She didn't let that one setback stop her from pursuing her vision of being the C.E.O of her own company and I'm so proud of her success. In that small and quick business venture, we really didn't lose anything but gained knowledge and wisdom we otherwise wouldn't have acquired.

As we take this journey together, I'm going to share with you the steps it took for me to reach my short list of accomplishments.

Life is hard and comes with enough challenges of its own and then you throw hopes, dreams, goals, and aspirations on top of the challenges; I can see chaos spinning around in your head right now but it doesn't have to be that hard.

I'm here to help you remove every obstacle and excuse from your mind. I'm here to help you conceptualize your dreams and go to the next level. Let's get started!

As we take this journey together, I'm going to share with you the steps it took for me to reach my short list of accomplishments.

PERMISSION TO DREAM

I love dreaming about places I want to go, people I want to meet and food I want to taste. I don't only dream about people, places and things that seem out of reach but I dream of better days in my life, days where joy seems unstoppable and peace walks through every room in my house. Sometimes I sit in my room and dream about being happy. Happy because there's no debt, I love my job, and my family in general, is doing well. I dream of having a big family who comes together for gatherings around great food and fun then, as I wake up from my dream and my knees begin to hurt, I dream about the pain disappearing.

We often think dreams must be big and huge but they are sometimes small. In fact, I believe the best dreams are those of little significance to others but mean the world to you personally. After all, dreams are private. They are intimate. They're tiny pieces of who you are deep down inside.

There's a young man who had not one dream but several dreams. He shared his dreams with his family and his father kept them hidden in his heart. Even though it took years for those dreams to become a reality, they did materialize and he was able to help provide for his family in the midst of hard times because he never lost hope of the manifestation of his dreams. Sure, there were ups and downs throughout the process of the young man's journey and at one point he was even thrown into prison but even then, he never gave up. He held on to his dream and most importantly, he didn't lose faith. Obstacles are going to always occur, that's just a part of life but how you respond is within your full control. The name of the young man is Joseph from the book of Genesis of the Bible. He is a great example of dreams coming true in the midst of chaos. What I love about his journey is how he never lost his focus but always kept his eyes on the expected outcome, which was for his dream to become reality. A lot of people are afraid to dream because they don't want to face difficulties that may arise while attempting to reach for their purpose. But how will you ever know whether you're going to be successful if you don't at least try.

Therefore, I give you full permission to dream. If you want to dream small that's okay but if you can, go ahead and dream big. There are no limits on dreaming. You can have as big or as small of a dream as you want. You can dream as many dreams as your spirit can hold and your mind can conceive. You can dream in black and white or dream in color, as long as you dream! There are no rules here and no one holding you back, except you. God wants you to have it all. When He gave us free will, it included the free will of dreaming whatever our heart so desires. The key is to allow your mind, spirit, and soul the freedom to create the next stage of your journey.

> I give you full permission to dream. If you want to dream small that's okay but if you can, go ahead and dream big.

When I talk to people much older than me and ask what their biggest regrets are in life, it's almost always the same response, "I wish I didn't let fear stop me from doing this…, that… or the other…." We blame fear but it's actually ourselves standing in the way of greatness. Move yourself out the way! In fact, look yourself in the mirror right now and say these words, "I am worthy, I am capable, I have no fear and I am unstoppable!" Repeat it over and over again, until it sinks deep down in your soul.

Listen to me and listen to me good, life is scary and unpredictable. I know firsthand as my life has shifted in many directions but I never let it sway me from the things I hold dearly in my heart. I've given my dreams no other option but to become a realization. Therefore, shake negativity off and bounce back quickly from whatever comes your way. You've got this! I believe in you and know God has deposited everything you need to be successful, so let's kick excuses aside and move forward.

Here's a tip: if you listen and obey God you will be blessed with prosperity throughout your life and all your years will be pleasant. As we know from scripture God doesn't put too many requirements on us. He asks us to be obedient, to listen to Him, acknowledge Him and, hold His voice above all other voices and follow His instructions.

A PLACE CALLED "HERE"

Anytime you feel like you have absolutely no idea of how you're going to make to the next payday or how you're going to pursue your purpose without financial backing, how you're going to make it another day in your mediocre job that you want to quit so bad, or how you're going to be the person you dream about; I want you to say this scripture to yourself. Personalize the word of God: "my God shall supply all my needs"- Philippians 4:19. God loves us so much, He's going to supply all our needs. He's not going to leave us hanging on a limb with no hope but instead everything we can imagine, He will fulfill.

"Here" is a place I know all too well. I'm comfortable "here." Everyone knows me "here." "Here" is where you're at right now in life and it feels good but it hurts just the same. "Here" feels good because it's a familiar place. It hurts to be "here" because you know there's more beyond where you are right now but you don't know how to go from "here" to "there". It's like you're reaching and stretching to grab something that will never exist. You kind of see it but you won't know for sure it's "there" until you actually touch and pull it in for confirmation.

First, I want you to know that I am fully invested in seeing you achieve your dreams. I know it must feel impossible. I know you must be looking around at your current circumstances and be wondering how can I create something out of nothing. I remember when my dream of writing a book looked unachievable. It seemed like a huge task and I didn't know where to start. I thought, even if I could publish a book, I didn't know if anyone would buy it and I wrestled with feeling unqualified to write on any level.

> I want you to know that I am
> fully invested in seeing you
> achieve your dreams.

Yet the urge to create my first book would not leave my spirit and slowly it began to occupy my every thought. To put myself out of the misery my dream was causing me, I just simply began to write. I knew I wanted to write a devotional book because I was already writing daily devotions and sending them to friends, which turned into a blog.

So, one day I decided to start with what I already had. Beginning with one page a night, I began to rewrite and edit my most popular devotions. The action of writing was my first step in going from "here" to "there", from a dream to manifestation. To put it very simply, start with what you already have and use what you already know to jumpstart the process of achieving your dreams.

What do you already possess that you can share with others? What are your skills? What are your talents? What do you love doing and can do very well? What do you want to try? What do you want to learn? What's missing or needed in your community?

Use this time and space to write down every gift, talent, and resource that comes to your mind. Write about your community, family, and friends. Use the information you already possess to build a list of needs that can possibly join together with your creativity. Don't think about what you don't have, only focus on what you do have and list it. Nothing is too small to list. If you love animals, write it down. If you love doing laundry, write it down. If you love to cook, write it down. If you love to sing, write it down. There's always someone out there who will pay you for your God-given talents and skills because they can't do what you do or don't have the patience to do it.

This is where we do what I call taking inventory of your gifts. By taking inventory, you're opening up your mind to all the possibilities that are out "there."

So, whatever gifts you've been blessed with, write it down, right now!

MY INVENTORY

_____
_____
_____
_____
_____
_____
_____
_____
_____
_____
_____
_____
_____
_____
_____
_____
_____
_____
_____
_____
_____
_____
_____
_____
_____

WHAT IS MY DREAM?

A few weeks ago, someone said to me, "God will give you whatever you ask for." For some reason, that baffled me and I didn't know what to ask for. If I could have anything in the world, what would it be? Many will say money! But money easily gotten is money easily spent. The idea of having a lot of money sounds good but if you don't know how to turn the money into more money, you'll be penniless in no time. So, instead, I began to ponder on what would last a really long time. Now, don't get me wrong. I would love to have an abundance of money but fortune without wisdom leads to poverty. Therefore, I asked God for the keys to success. Success can't be spent. You can't trade it, you can't borrow it, and you can't buy it. You either have it or you don't. I want to give you an opportunity to think about your dreams in connection with your inventory list.

What is it you want or need or would like to have and experience? Where would you like to be this time next year? What have you always wanted to do? What is it you feel you do really well, better than most people? What do you like to do and can see yourself doing every day?

Use this time and space to really look into what you want and the direction you want your life to go. Drop all the fear, doubt, and anxiety. No one is going to say, "you can't do it!" because this time is just for you and your dreams. Remember, I said dreams are intimate. They are personal and you don't have to share your dreams with anyone unless you want to, otherwise, they are your secret. Hold on to them as tight as you can.

If you are going to share your dream, share with someone of the same like mind, with the same determination, so that together you can encourage each other. Two is better than one; the two of you will strengthen each other and hold one another accountable. However, be wise in giving someone a glimpse into your dream because if you tell the wrong person, it could cause jealousy instead of inspiration. Nevertheless, whether you keep your dreams to yourself or share them with someone, I want you to begin using your imagination and creativity to form a vision.

Now, close your eyes and begin to dream. Keep your eyes closed for 3 minutes, then open them and write down whatever you envision in the space provided below.

Ready, set, dream!

MY DREAM

_____

_____

_____

_____

_____

_____

_____

_____

_____

_____

_____

_____

_____

_____

_____

_____

_____

_____

_____

_____

_____

_____

_____

_____

_____

JOURNEY TO A DREAM!

On my journey to becoming a published book author, I knew nothing at first. I knew absolutely nothing about the process of writing, editing, printing, or getting the book in stores. All I knew is that I had a dream and I wanted to see that dream manifest. So, to familiarize myself with the book industry, I began to look at every type of book I could get my hands on. What did I look for? I looked at how they were made. I looked at the different book covers to see what stood out and what didn't. I looked at the interior of the book for the letter type. I looked at the paper used. I looked at the various sizes to see what were more popular. I studied every aspect of every book I owned. I even looked at how the book was arranged with chapter headings and introductions. I wanted my book to look like it was meant to sit on a shelf amongst some of the high-quality large publishing company books.

I still remember the day I got a call from my book distributor asking me for a case of books for one of the largest bookstores. They had called and asked for my book by name. A few months afterward, I was able to walk into Barnes and Nobel's and see my book on the shelf. It's one of the highlights of my career but it only happened because I had a dream for greatness. I didn't know how it was going to manifest but I trust God to manifest it.

If you can dream it, you can achieve it. Yes, the road is going to be rough but the prize is never out of reach. You have to be determined and always keep your dream in the forefront your mind. Your dream is not just going to pop up out of thin air. You are going to have to do your homework to make your dream materialize. What is the homework? The homework for me was going through every book and noting every detail I wanted to incorporate into my own book.

> You are going to have to do your homework to make your dream materialize.

This is where you begin to examine and take notice of any and everything that is similar or comes close to what you want to do or make. Let's say you decide that you love lotion. You love the way it smells, how it makes your skin look and feel. However, you notice that in your location there aren't a lot of options for lotions with different scents and you don't see any locally made lotions with natural ingredients. Also, what's available in your area is all imported, which makes it more expensive.

So, what is your first step? The first thing you do is gather some lotion samples. You don't have to buy them, just find some empty ones, ask family and friends for their bottles when they are done using it. Then, take note of every ingredient in the bottle. Now, most commercial lotions are going to have ingredients that you won't be able to use because the chemicals can't be purchased by the average person but there are plenty of natural substitutes you can use in its place.

Once you have your list of ingredients, collect some of the items to start making a few samples of the lotion. You're not going to get the lotion right the first time and that's okay. I don't expect you to get it right but I do expect you to continue trying and experimenting until you produce something tangible. There are many things we use today that were actually created for another purpose. I met someone at an entrepreneur workshop who tried to make deodorant but it came out too soft, yet creamy. Did she give up? Did she throw the first batch of deodorant in the garbage and start over? No, her boyfriend saw what she didn't and applied it to his face and used it as shaving cream - Wa-lah! She put the shaving cream in a bottle and started selling it and people bought it.

From her initial failure, a new solution was birthed. All because she saw opportunity instead of failure, so don't be afraid to fail. It's a part of the process. As you begin to research and analyze what it's going to take to make your dream come true, I want you to begin writing down all the necessary ingredients as you discover them.

My mother loved making cakes and was really good at it. In fact, she was so good at baking that she became known as, "The Cake Lady." It hardly took any effort for her to wake up and make a cake. It didn't take any effort because she knew the key essential ingredients needed to make any cake: eggs, milk, butter, flour, and sugar, at the very least. Those ingredients were her foundation or "go to" recipe. What we are doing here is laying the foundation in which your dreams are going to be built upon. This foundation is going to allow you to see your dreams manifest into something tangible. It was with the key baking ingredients that my mother worked by day and baked by night to put me through private school. She turned her passion for baking into a part-time money-making business. Let's not waste any more time; use the space below to begin to list the key ingredients you're going to need to bring every dream you have to manifestation.

Along with the key ingredients, also include: key people you need to meet, key places you need to visit, and don't neglect to mention any key help that's needed. Don't be intimidated by the key ingredients. Remember – it's only eggs, butter, sugar, and flour, at the very least. My point is if you see them as impossible ingredients then you won't continue with boldness. This is where faith has to kick in and you have to know that someone has the 1 egg or the cup of sugar you need and they are just waiting for you to knock on their door and say, "can I borrow a cup of sugar, my cake depends on it."

There are a lot of people that have the information you need on your journey to dream manifestation and they are more than willing to share what they know. However, in order for you to gain more insight, experience, knowledge, and assistance, you can't be afraid to reach out to those who may be an expert in what you're trying to do. Although you may get some no's, don't let that stop you. A "no" today can lead to a "yes" tomorrow. Keep knocking and eventually, a door shall open. Any "no" just means they're not aligned with your journey and God has a better resource as you continue down the path.

Now let's start writing those key ingredients down and don't be stingy, list everything you're going to need. I most recently wrote down that I want a building as my key ingredient to doing ministry and running my businesses. I have no idea where the building is coming from but I'm not afraid to write it down and believe that somehow God is going to meet my need. I have no fear, therefore I'm unstoppable. When I was putting my first book together, I needed a book cover. I wrote it down as one of my key ingredients to publish my book and began to search the internet for a graphic designer and I found one who specialized in Christian book covers. At the time, I had no idea how to pull this off but I had a vision and it had to come to pass. As I took the first step, God began to work things out on my behalf.

As for the building for ministry and business, who knew God would bless me with a 3000 square feet house to start my church and enough room for a home office. I asked for a building but wasn't specific enough. So, I got an all in one house. I can't complain because the house is beautiful and now I'm believing God for many more great things. Therefore, I want you to be very descriptive and detailed. Cross every "t" in laying out what you need to get started,

Everything you need in life is just waiting for you to stake a claim on it!

KEY INGREDIENTS

_____
_____
_____
_____
_____
_____
_____
_____
_____
_____
_____
_____
_____
_____
_____
_____
_____
_____
_____
_____
_____
_____
_____
_____

MIXING IT ALL TOGETHER

Let's take a look back at all the hard work you've done so far. You've thought long and hard about what it is you want to achieve, thus writing down your dreams. You understand achieving your dream doesn't have to be so complicated.

You can start right where you are, with exactly what you already have. As you continue to do your homework and research for other key ingredients to add with what you already have, you're also compiling a list of key people, places and things needed to go to the next level. On this path, it's not going to be easy. I feel a need to emphasize this because many begin the journey of entrepreneurship but very few follow-thru and even fewer are actually successful and making a living at working for themselves. Yet, remember what I've said previously, don't be afraid of failure. Ten failures have led to one inspirational success story.

I talked about my mother in the previous chapter, who worked for a company by day and baked by night. Some may think she wasn't successful because she never became a full-time baker in her own establishment. Yet, what I failed to mention was how much she loved her job as a social worker and had a gift for loving on people. Therefore, she had the best of both worlds and was compensated for both. Compensation by way of money is after all, what we're all looking for in the end but I warn you to not let it define your success. If you don't make any money the first six months, first year, or even next 3 years, don't get discouraged and feel defeated. Every day your business is open, every day you're doing what you love, every time you obtain a new client, every day can produce a product and complete a service; you're a success story.

Success not should be measured solely by how much money you make. For instance, I've sold a lot of books but I'm not rich or wealthy but my reward is not in the book sales. My reward is when someone reads my book and it changes their life. If you pick up this book, complete every chapter, then go start living your dreams, then I am successful because of what you accomplished. You are what I care about and what defines my success. If I never sell another book but one person says, "I'm better because of what you said in chapter 5," then I'm happy. That means I have completed the task God has given me.

Therefore, don't just fix your eyes on financial gain but always incorporate other ways to gauge and measure success. This way you won't feel discouraged and give up as soon as the money doesn't come rolling in. Birthing a dream takes time and plenty of patience. Don't get weary in well doing; it's all going to come together because you're putting the effort in right now.

NOW YOU HAVE A PLAN!

I admit that I am the worst at sitting down and writing out a plan but lucky for you; you've already done the work up front, so now we just have to put it all together and structure the content.

In a few sentences, what is the overall idea of your dream?

_____

_____

_____

_____

_____

_____

_____

_____

_____

How will your dream help your family, people or your community?

_____

_____

_____

_____

_____

_____

_____

Who will buy into your dream? (support you, purchase your goods or services)

_____

_____

_____

_____

_____

_____

_____

How much will you charge people?

_____

_____

_____

_____

_____

_____

How will you get paid for your service or product?

_____

_____

_____

_____

_____

_____

_____

How else will you be compensated from your dream? (Outside of money, meaning: changing someone's life)

_____

_____

_____

_____

_____

_____

How will family, friends, and the community find out about your dream? (Word of mouth, flyers, posters, etc.)

_____

_____

_____

_____

_____

_____

How can you encourage people to support your dream?

_____

_____

_____

_____

_____

_____

_____

What are some specific obstacles, challenges, concerns or questions?

1.
_____

2.
_____

3.
_____

4.
_____

5.
_____

Solutions to your obstacles, challenges, concerns and questions:

1.

_____

2.

_____

3.

_____

4.

_____

5.

_____

Your dream will be successful when you achieve these results:

Number of customers:

_____

Or
Annual/monthly income:

_____

Or
Type of impact:

_____

Or
Other level of achievement:

_____

See, it's all over with. Now that wasn't so bad, was it? I don't think so and it forced you to really look at the great gifts and resources God has already given you. You have exactly what you need to get started. You don't have to get started with a perfect product or service. You don't need to bring in expert assistance right off the back but get started with what you already have and use those who are eager to support and help where needed. As your business grows and matures, you will grow the brand and take it to new levels, increasing the quality, step-by-step but you must launch out and simply get started. Progress will come as you continue to in the hard work.

Success is not built overnight. It takes hard work, perseverance, and dedication; all of which you've already shown you have and I'm so excited to be a part of your phenomenal journey.

Congratulations to you for taking this step in pursuing your dreams. The universe is working with you and not against you. God is orchestrating everything in your favor to take you to the next level.

Ready, set, leap!

WHAT TO DO NEXT?

Now that you have a plan in place it's time to execute. Please don't let fear creep in and steal your enthusiasm. There's nothing to fear, you're already a success because you've made it this far.

The next step is to take one goal at a time with your new action plan. Prioritize what's needed first. With my book, I composed all the pages. I knew I needed content, so it was my first priority. I Then went step-by-step until the finished product was in my living room waiting to hit the shelves.

The best part about pursuing your dreams in this generation is access to immediate information. Read many books, youtube and network with as many people as possible will serve you good. Information is your friend and at your disposal – use it.

Take advantage of your friends and family by using them as guinea pigs. I passed my first manuscript draft off to fellow church members, friends, and family for frequent feedback, corrections, and ideas.

Remain open to honest criticism. Not everyone is a hater trying to put out your entrepreneurial light. Believe God for people who want to see you go to the next level and willing to invest their time in helping to progress you. Also, just because someone recommends it, doesn't mean you have to use the advice. Thank the person and trust your gut feeling with how to craft your finished product.

CEASE THE OPPORTUNITY!

On her way home from work, a woman discovered a house she absolutely loved it. It was the right size, beautiful entryway, circluar drive and quiet community – everything she ever dreamed. Every day for a year she would drive through the neighborhood and look at the house, praying God would give her the opportunity to one day own it. Something inside of her felt it was perfect for her needs, close to her job and would be such a blessing. Yet, she never did anything about it.

Another woman, while walking by the same house noticed an elderly man putting up a for sale sign. She stopped and looked at the house, only to ponder why he was selling such a beautiful home. As she stood there, the elderly man approached her. He asked, "Do you like my house?" She responded, "Yes, it's beautiful but why are you selling it?" He responds, "my wife passed away last year and my children no longer want me to stay in the house all alone. Therefore, they are sending for me to come live with them in another state. If you love the house, you can have it for $5. At this point, I just want to get rid of it and move on with the rest of my life." The woman gave the man $5.

The Other woman while completing here daily tour of the neighborhood, noticed the new owner coming out of the house. They locked eyes and the new owner waves hello. The woman stops this time and compliments the house. As they strike up a conversation, the women gather's the courage to state, "every day I cruise through this neighborhood in awe of such a beautiful house and ask God for the opportunity to one day to own it." The new owner responds, "Well, that's interesting because I often feel as if this house doesn't belong to me but should belong to someone else."

Don't let someone else live your dream! You have what it takes to get what you want. In case you still don't feel confident, I want you to repeat these affirmations to yourself every day, as often as possible. Post them on your mirror, in the car, and around your house. Immerse your subconscious with these words to kick-start your drive for success.

- I deserve success!
- Success and wealth are attracted to me.
- I have a constant flow of creativity.
- The right people are joining my path to success.
- I have more than enough to achieve my goals.
- I have all the faith I need to go to the next level.
- The spirit of abundance is opening new doors.
- I achieve my goals easily.
- I am worthy!
- New opportunities are coming my way.
- God is working on my behalf.
- God is aligning me with divine resources.

I constantly repeat affirmations of faith to keep my mind occupied with positive energy. When negativity tries to creep in, I simply turn up the volume, and before you know it I see results.

NOTES